you ARE loved

To my forever family. I love you! —Sofia Sanchez

For my grandchildren. —Meg O'Hair

To my family. —Sofia Cardoso

Photo credits: page 37 (top left): © Melissa Babasin Photography; page 37 (top right): © Jennifer Varanini Sanchez; page 37 (center): © Tiffany Green Photography & Designs; page 37 (bottom left): © Melissa Babasin Photography; page 37 (bottom right): © Jennifer Varanini Sanchez.

No part of this publication may be reproduced, stored in a retrieval system, or transmitted in any form or by any means, electronic, mechanical, photocopying, recording, or otherwise, without written permission of the publisher. For information regarding permission, write to Scholastic Inc., Attention: Permissions Department, 557 Broadway, New York, NY 10012.

ISBN 978-1-338-89377-9

Text copyright © 2023 by Margaret O'Hair. Illustrations copyright © 2023 by Scholastic Inc. All rights reserved. Published by Scholastic Inc., *Publishers since 1920.* SCHOLASTIC and associated logos are trademarks and/or registered trademarks of Scholastic Inc.

The publisher does not have any control over and does not assume any responsibility for author or third-party websites or their content.

12 11 10 9 8 7 6 5 4 3 2 1   23 24 25 26 27 28

Printed in the U.S.A.   40

This edition first printing, January 2023

Book design by Katie Fitch

Edited by Samantha Swank

A BOOK ABOUT FAMILIES

Inspired by
SOFIA SANCHEZ

Written by Margaret O'Hair   Illustrated by Sofia Cardoso

SCHOLASTIC INC.

My name is Sofia Sanchez. I live with my parents, my three older brothers, two dogs, and an orange kitty. Diego is my oldest brother. Mateo is the second oldest in my family. Joaquin is next. He is just one year older than me! They are my family.

My three brothers were born into my family. But I came into my family in a different way. My parents saw a picture of me when I was in an orphanage in Ukraine. I was just one year old.

My parents knew I was supposed to be in the Sanchez family. They traveled all the way across the globe to meet me. My mom and dad adopted me, and I chose them right back. That's how we became a family.

But my family is more than just the people I live with. I have family spread out all over the world!

My dad is named Hector. He was born in Mexico. I have many aunts, uncles, and cousins who still live there. We get to visit them a lot!

My mom's name is Jennifer. She was born in California. My grandparents live in the same town as us, and I have more aunts, uncles, and cousins nearby.

My family and I have lots of adventures together. We travel to new places, visit movie theaters and water parks, and go bowling and horseback riding. We hike and swim and walk our dogs.

Your family probably looks different from mine. That's okay, because all families are different. And there's not just one way to make a family. What matters is that you and your family love one another—just like mine does!

Most of all you are loved by your family.

No one loves you like your family loves you.

But what makes a family?

Family isn't just the people you are related to or the people you see every day.

Families are made with **LOVE**.

A family is something special. No two families look the same.

Sometimes you are born into your family.

Sometimes you choose your family.

And sometimes your family chooses you.

Family is the people who are important to you—the people who love you just the way you are.

Families can be loud or quiet.

They can be big

or small

or somewhere in between.

Sometimes the people in a family look the same.

Other families are made up of
lots of different kinds of people.

There's no right or wrong way to be a family.
What keeps a family together is LOVE.

Some families are lucky to live together under one roof.

Other families may be spread out across a neighborhood, a country, or the world.

But family is about more than where you live.

Families are people who love and care for one another.

So even when you're away from your family,

you still carry them with you in your heart.

Some families spend lots of time together.

They celebrate together.

They eat and play and work together.

They know that they'll always be there to support one another, no matter what.

But families are not perfect.

Sometimes families **ARGUE**,

get **MAD**, and get **SAD**.

Loving people can be hard.

But being a family means promising to make up and try again.

Families grow and change.

Babies are born

and kids grow up.

We meet new people who become part of our families.

And sometimes we lose people we love, too.

But no matter what your family looks like, one thing stays the same: how much you LOVE one another.

Parents, grandparents, and siblings.

Aunts, uncles, and cousins.

Friends, teachers, and neighbors.

Life is so much better when you have people to love—
and people who love you—by your side.

There's not just one way to make a family.

Families are born when you find the people who make you HAPPY and help you feel STRONG.

A Note From Sofia's Mom

For as long as I can remember, all I ever wanted to be was a mom. I love children. I love family. I was so excited to create a family of my own.

I was blessed with three biological boys. It wasn't until giving birth to Joaquin, who has Down syndrome, that I realized there are children who don't have a family solely because they have a disability. That's when we opened our eyes to the possibility of adoption for our family.

Families are always changing, and ours changed when we found Sofia. When she came into our family, it was like she was always meant to be with us. We all fit together, and I can't imagine life any other way.

We are so lucky to have a community around us that has loved and supported us from the beginning. It truly takes a village, and when you do life right, your village can become family—the people you go to when life gets hard, and when you have moments to celebrate!

Thank you for being part of our family.

—Jennifer

FAMILY

MARGARET "MEG" O'HAIR

is a mom to two kids, a kindergarten teacher, and an award-winning writer. She likes to be on the water—whether it's on boats, kayaks, or paddleboards—with her family and their three Portuguese water dogs. Meg has been inspired to write books about Sofia from the first day they met, including their previous picture book, *You Are Enough*. *You Are Loved* is her ninth book for children. Meg can be found at margaretohair.com, on Instagram at @margaretohair, and on YouTube at Margaret O'Hair, where she creates fun educational videos for kids.

SOFIA CARDOSO

is a Portuguese illustrator, designer, and foodie whose passion for illustration goes all the way back to her childhood years. Nowadays, using a mix of both traditional and digital mediums, she enjoys whimsical storytelling and drawing young characters. Her sweet and colorful illustrations featured in children's books and licensed art aim to spark joy, with a pinch or two of magic. She also loves cooking, baking, at-home yoga, and all things Christmas. She can be found on Instagram and Twitter at @sofiagcardosoo and online at *sofiacardoso.com*.